ACCENT ON ACHIEVEMENT

A comprehensive band method that develops creativity and musicianship

Dear Band Student:

Congratulations on deciding to become a member of the **band**! There is a special kind of enjoyment that comes from performing with a musical group that can be found nowhere else. As a skilled band musician, you will be able to play a wide variety of musical styles from **symphony** to **jazz**, from **contemporary pop** to **marching band**. With regular daily practice, there's no limit to the exciting musical experiences waiting for you! We wish you the best of success in achieving your musical goals.

John O'Reilly   *Mark Williams*

John O'Reilly   Mark Williams

Illustrations: Martin Ledyard
Photography (pages 3 & 4): Jordan Miller

Instrument photos (cover, pages 1 & 2) are courtesy of Yamaha Corporation of America.
Thanks to the students and staff of Lindero Canyon Middle School and Band Director Matt McKagan for their participation in the photographs on pages 3 and 4.

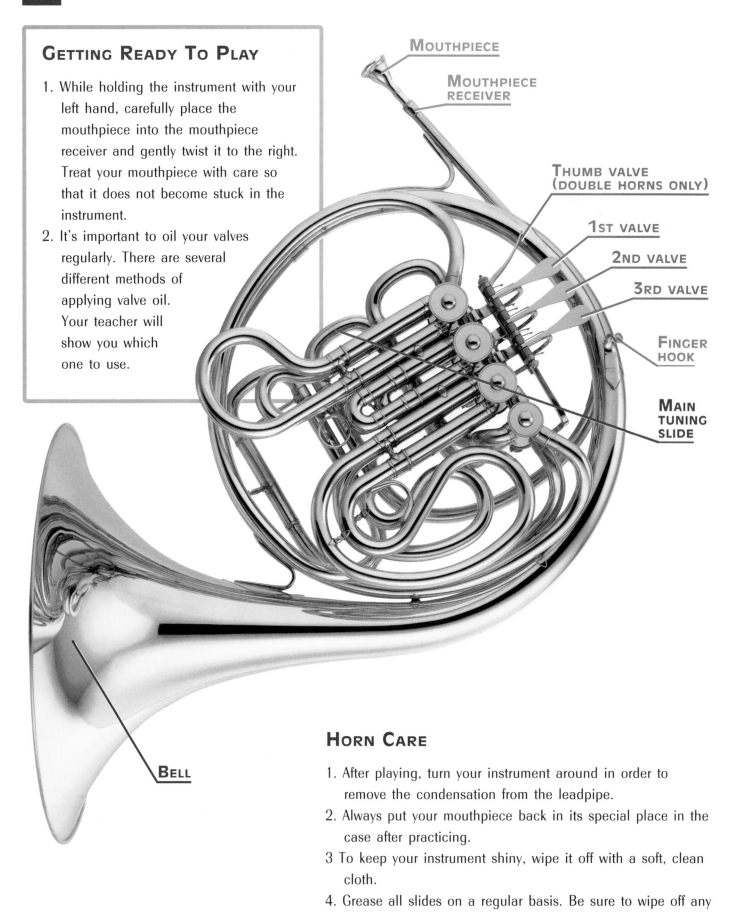

GETTING READY TO PLAY

1. While holding the instrument with your left hand, carefully place the mouthpiece into the mouthpiece receiver and gently twist it to the right. Treat your mouthpiece with care so that it does not become stuck in the instrument.

2. It's important to oil your valves regularly. There are several different methods of applying valve oil. Your teacher will show you which one to use.

MOUTHPIECE

MOUTHPIECE RECEIVER

THUMB VALVE (DOUBLE HORNS ONLY)

1ST VALVE

2ND VALVE

3RD VALVE

FINGER HOOK

MAIN TUNING SLIDE

BELL

HORN CARE

1. After playing, turn your instrument around in order to remove the condensation from the leadpipe.

2. Always put your mouthpiece back in its special place in the case after practicing.

3 To keep your instrument shiny, wipe it off with a soft, clean cloth.

4. Grease all slides on a regular basis. Be sure to wipe off any excess slide grease.

5. Store only those items in your case that the case is designed to hold. Forcing music or other objects into your horn case can cause problems with the instrument.

6. If your mouthpiece should become stuck, please seek the assistance of your band director or music dealer, who have a special tool needed to remove it without damage.

CHECK YOUR PLAYING POSITION

1. Sit on the front half of your chair.
2. Keep your feet flat on the floor.
3. Sit up straight and tall.
4. The bell of your horn rests on your right leg.
5. Place your left thumb in the ring or on the B♭ thumb valve and your left hand little finger in the hook. Keeping your fingers curved, touch the valves with the tips of your other three fingers.
6. Cup your right hand, keeping your fingers and thumb together. Place your cupped hand inside the bell with the back of our fingers resting on the bottom. Your hand should cover approximately one-half of the opening.

FORMING THE EMBOUCHURE

Embouchure (ahm'-buh-sure) is a French word used to describe the way you shape your mouth while playing. Here is how to form a good embouchure:

1. Moisten your lips and bring them together as if you're saying the letter "M".
2. Keeping your jaw open and relaxed, firm up the corners of your lips to form a slightly puckered smile.
3. While the corners of your lips are firm, the center of your lips should stay relaxed for the best sound.

PRODUCING YOUR FIRST TONE

1. Practice taking a full breath, filling the bottom of your lungs so that your stomach expands. Then fill the top of your lungs without raising your shoulders. With gentle pressure, exhale completely. Always using a full breath while playing helps to produce long, full tones.
2. Our first tone will be produced using just the mouthpiece. Center the mouthpiece on your lips, remembering to keep the corners of your lips firm. Take a deep breath through the corners of your mouth, then buzz through the mouthpiece starting with the syllable "Tah". Make the tone last as long as possible. Next, produce a "siren" on your mouthpiece, making the sound go up and down smoothly several times by changing the size of the opening in the middle of your lips.

PRACTICE TIPS

1. Try to find a place with a good, firm chair where you will not be interrupted. Use a music stand to hold your music in the correct position for playing.
2. Start by playing long tones. This builds your embouchure and improves your tone.
3. Always include some already learned "review" pieces, so that you continue to improve and perfect your performance.
4. Spend a concentrated period of time on the most difficult parts of your music. Avoid the temptation to play only the easy parts.
5. In addition to your regular practice, spend some time each day buzzing on your mouthpiece. Practicing sirens and even trying to play familiar songs on just the mouthpiece will make you a better player on your instrument.
6. To make your practice even more enjoyable, try playing along with the *ACCENT ON ACHIEVEMENT* accompaniment CDs or cassettes.

THE STAFF

5 lines and 4 spaces used for writing music.

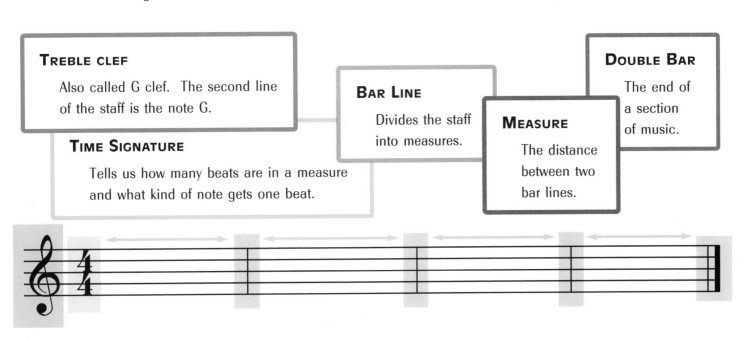

TREBLE CLEF

Also called G clef. The second line of the staff is the note G.

TIME SIGNATURE

Tells us how many beats are in a measure and what kind of note gets one beat.

BAR LINE

Divides the staff into measures.

MEASURE

The distance between two bar lines.

DOUBLE BAR

The end of a section of music.

THE MUSICAL ALPHABET

The musical alphabet uses only the letters A through G. These are used to name the notes on the staff in **LINE-SPACE-LINE-SPACE** order (A, B, C, D, E, F, G, A, B, etc.). There are rules that help us remember the names of the lines and spaces of the staff.

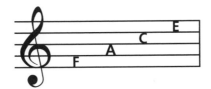

From bottom to top, the spaces spell **FACE**.

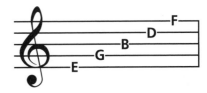

The lines can be remembered by using the first letter of each word in the sentence **Every Good Boy Does Fine.**

LEDGER LINES

Used to extend the staff.

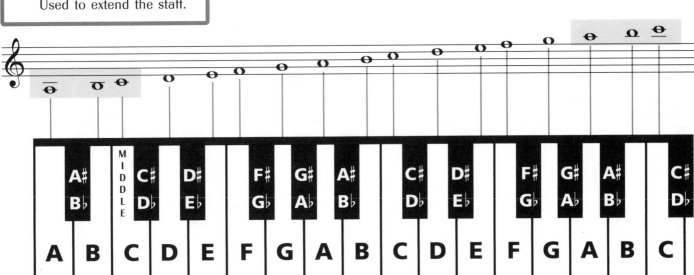

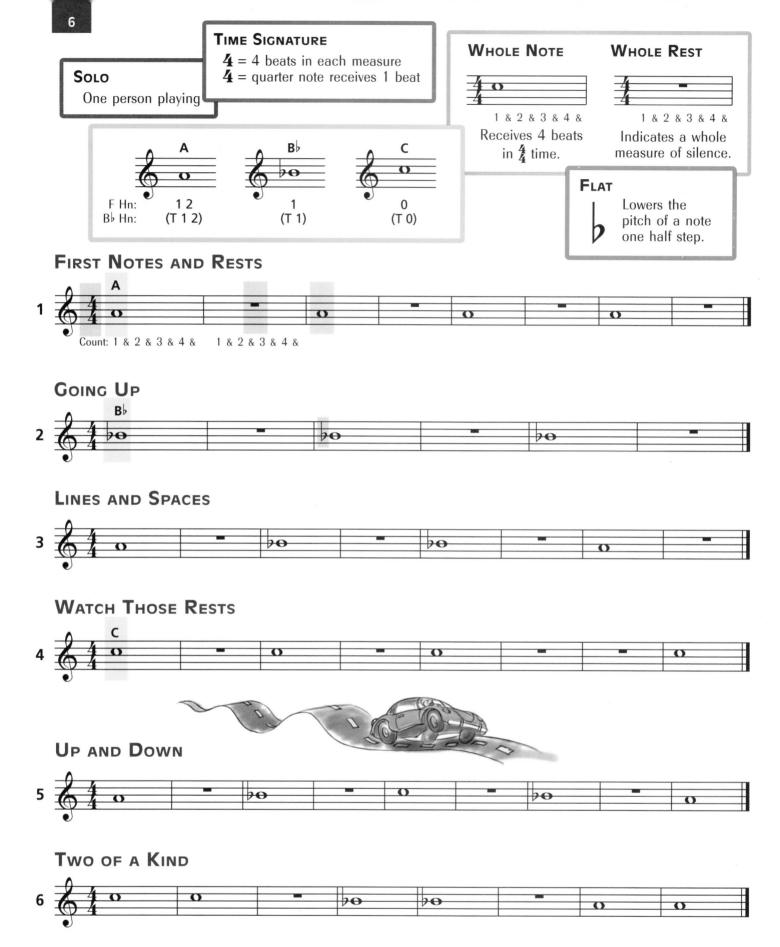

FIRST NOTES AND RESTS

GOING UP

LINES AND SPACES

WATCH THOSE RESTS

UP AND DOWN

TWO OF A KIND

ACCENT ON LISTENING

Listen carefully to the soloist, then match the pitch.

SOLO BAND SOLO BAND SOLO BAND SOLO BAND

SOLO
One person playing

TIME SIGNATURE
$\frac{4}{4}$ = 4 beats in each measure
$\frac{4}{4}$ = quarter note receives 1 beat

WHOLE NOTE

1 & 2 & 3 & 4 &
Receives 4 beats in $\frac{4}{4}$ time.

WHOLE REST

1 & 2 & 3 & 4 &
Indicates a whole measure of silence.

	E	F	G
F Hn:	0	1	0
B♭ Hn:	(2)	(0)	(1)

FIRST NOTES AND RESTS

1

Count: 1 & 2 & 3 & 4 &   1 & 2 & 3 & 4 &

E

GOING UP

2

F

LINES AND SPACES

3

WATCH THOSE RESTS

4

G

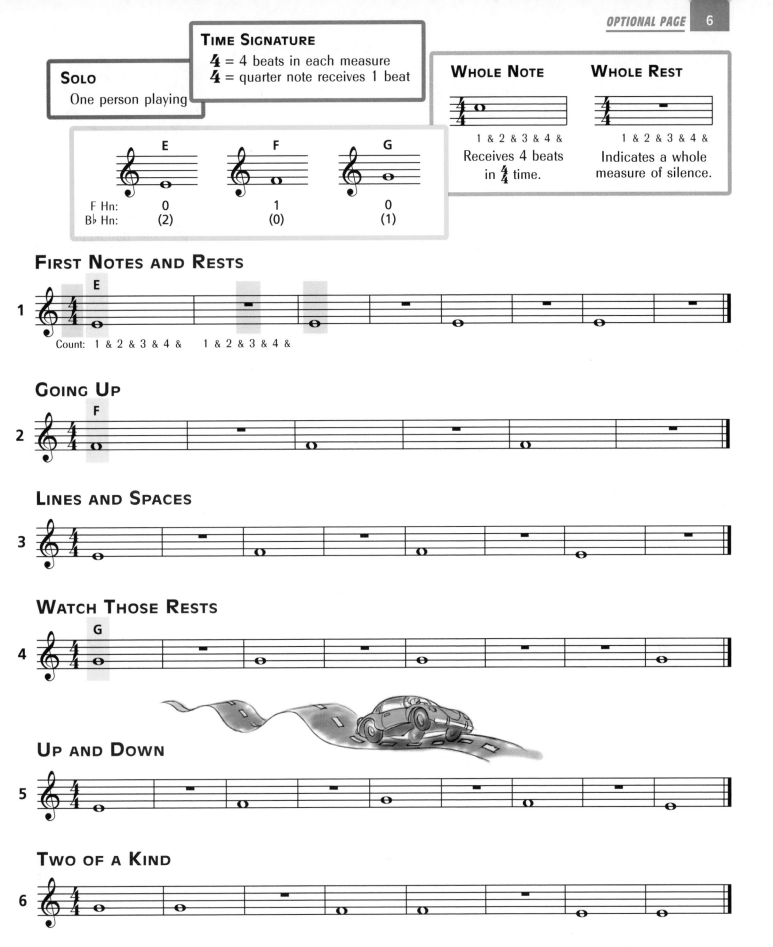

UP AND DOWN

5

TWO OF A KIND

6

ACCENT ON LISTENING

Listen carefully to the soloist, then match the pitch.

7

SOLO   BAND   SOLO   BAND   SOLO   BAND   SOLO   BAND

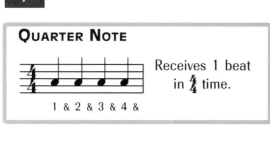

QUARTER NOTE

Receives 1 beat in **4/4** time.

1 & 2 & 3 & 4 &

DUET

A composition with parts for two players.

BREATH MARK ,

A suggested place to take a breath.

GOOD NEIGHBORS

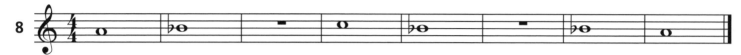

MIX 'EM UP

FOUR IN A ROW

Also B♭

Count: 1 & 2 & 3 & 4 &

PASSING NOTES (Duet)

TAKE FIVE

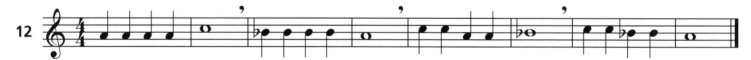

THREE-NOTE SAMBA

ACCENT ON THEORY   Fill in the note names, then fill in the fingerings.

Note name: ____

Fingering: _____

QUARTER NOTE

Receives 1 beat in 4/4 time.

1 & 2 & 3 & 4 &

BREATH MARK ,
A suggested place to take a breath.

DUET
A composition with parts for two players.

GOOD NEIGHBORS

8

MIX 'EM UP

9

FOUR IN A ROW

10

Count: 1 & 2 & 3 & 4 &

PASSING NOTES (Duet)

a
11
b

TAKE FIVE

12

THREE-NOTE SAMBA

13

ACCENT ON THEORY   Fill in the note names, then fill in the fingerings.

14

Note name: ____   ____   ____   ____   ____   ____

Fingering: ____   ____   ____   ____   ____   ____

HALF NOTE   **HALF REST**

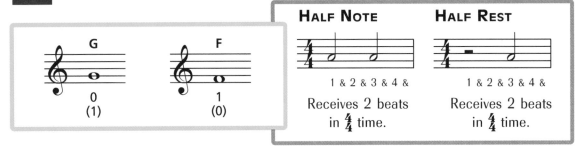

1 & 2 & 3 & 4 &   1 & 2 & 3 & 4 &

Receives 2 beats in 4/4 time.   Receives 2 beats in 4/4 time.

MOVIN' ON DOWN

HALF FULL OR HALF EMPTY (Duet)

HOT CROSS BUNS

English Folk Song

AU CLAIRE DE LA LUNE

French Folk Song

JINGLE BELLS

Traditional Carol

ACCENT ON LISTENING

1. Play "Mary Had a Little Lamb" by ear.
2. Write in the missing notes to complete the song.

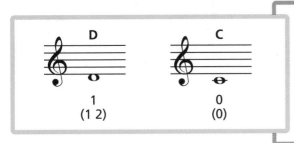

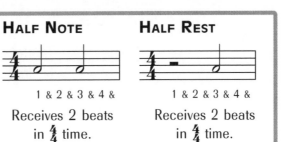

HALF NOTE   **HALF REST**

1 & 2 & 3 & 4 &   1 & 2 & 3 & 4 &

Receives 2 beats in 4/4 time.   Receives 2 beats in 4/4 time.

MOVIN' ON DOWN

HALF FULL OR HALF EMPTY (Duet)

Count: 1 & 2 & 3 & 4 &   1 & 2 & 3 & 4 &

HOT CROSS BUNS

English Folk Song

AU CLAIRE DE LA LUNE

French Folk Song

JINGLE BELLS

Traditional Carol

ACCENT ON LISTENING

1. Play "Mary Had a Little Lamb" by ear.
2. Write in the missing notes to complete the song.

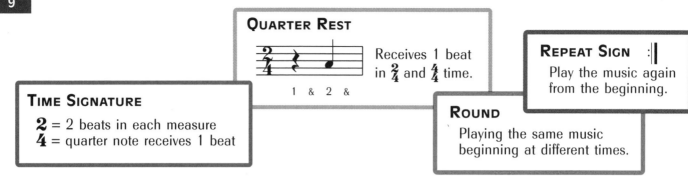

Quarter Rest
Receives 1 beat in 2/4 and 4/4 time.

1 & 2 &

Time Signature
2 = 2 beats in each measure
4 = quarter note receives 1 beat

Repeat Sign :|
Play the music again from the beginning.

Round
Playing the same music beginning at different times.

Handclapper's March

Better Than the Rest
Clap first, then play.

Good King Wenceslas
Traditional Carol

Donkey Round
American Folk Song

Dreydl, Dreydl
Traditional Hanukkah Song

Accent on French Horn

QUARTER REST

Receives 1 beat in 2/4 and 4/4 time.

1 & 2 &

TIME SIGNATURE

2 = 2 beats in each measure
4 = quarter note receives 1 beat

REPEAT SIGN :|

Play the music again from the beginning.

ROUND

Playing the same music beginning at different times.

HANDCLAPPER'S MARCH

a

21

Count: 1 & 2 &   1 & 2 &   1 & 2 &

Clap:

b

BETTER THAN THE REST

Clap first, then play.

22

GOOD KING WENCESLAS

Traditional Carol

23

DONKEY ROUND

American Folk Song

24 ①

②

DREYDL, DREYDL

Traditional Hanukkah Song

25

ACCENT ON FRENCH HORN

26

For more individual technique practice, see page 42, #1.

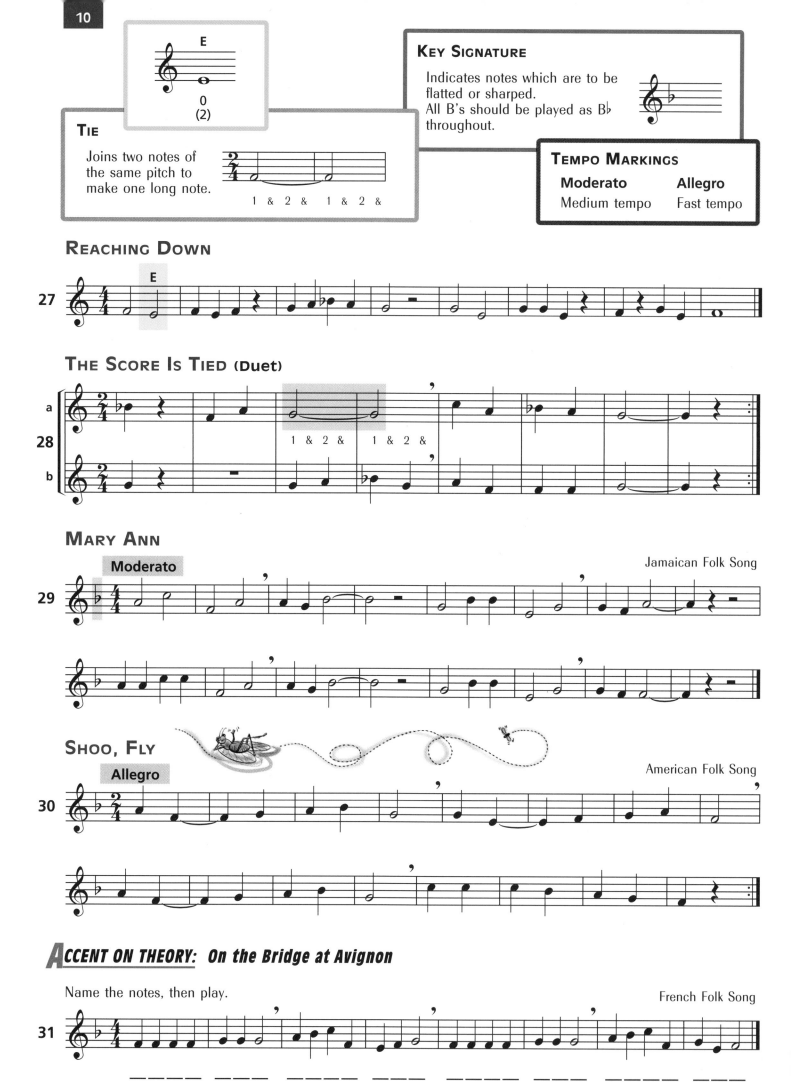

TIE

Joins two notes of the same pitch to make one long note.

KEY SIGNATURE

Indicates notes which are to be flatted or sharped. All B's should be played as B♭ throughout.

TEMPO MARKINGS

Moderato
Medium tempo

Allegro
Fast tempo

REACHING DOWN

27

THE SCORE IS TIED (Duet)

28

MARY ANN

Jamaican Folk Song

29

SHOO, FLY

American Folk Song

30

ACCENT ON THEORY: On the Bridge at Avignon

Name the notes, then play.

French Folk Song

31

TIE

Joins two notes of the same pitch to make one long note.

KEY SIGNATURE

Indicates notes which are to be flatted or sharped. Your first key signature contains no flats or sharps.

TEMPO MARKINGS

Moderato — Medium tempo

Allegro — Fast tempo

REACHING DOWN

27

THE SCORE IS TIED (Duet)

28 a
b

MARY ANN

Jamaican Folk Song

Moderato

29

SHOO, FLY

American Folk Song

Allegro

30

ACCENT ON THEORY: On the Bridge at Avignon

Name the notes, then play.

French Folk Song

31

ACCENT ON PERFORMANCE

HOLIDAY SAMPLER

Arr. by John O'Reilly
and Mark Williams

ACCENT ON PERFORMANCE

HOLIDAY SAMPLER

Arr. by John O'Reilly
and Mark Williams

Allegro

C

0
(0)

EIGHTH NOTES

Receive ½ beat in $\frac{2}{4}$ and $\frac{4}{4}$ time.

1 & 2 &

TEMPO MARKING
Andante
Moderately slow tempo

VARIATION
Changing the rhythm or notes of a theme to create variety.

EIGHTH-NOTE EXPRESS

32

Count: 1 & 2 & 3 & 4 &

RHYTHM RIDDLE

Clap first, then play.

33

BILE THEM CABBAGE DOWN

American Fiddle Tune

Allegro

34

SURPRISE SYMPHONY

Franz Joseph Haydn
(1732–1809)

THEME
Andante

35

VARIATION

ACCENT ON CREATIVITY: *Variation on Lightly Row*

Create your own variation by changing some of the quarter notes into pairs of eighth notes.

German Folk Song

36

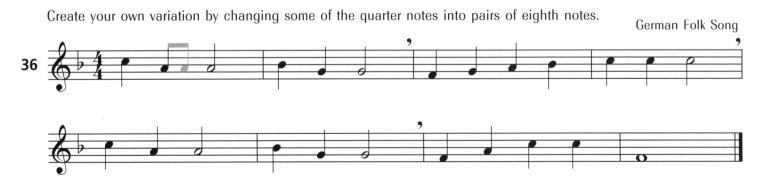

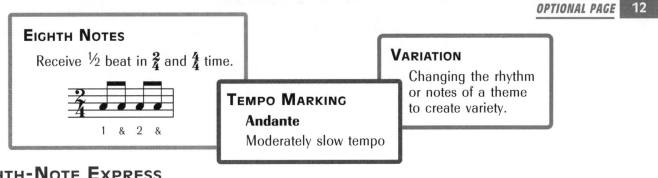

EIGHTH NOTES

Receive ½ beat in $\frac{2}{4}$ and $\frac{4}{4}$ time.

TEMPO MARKING
Andante
Moderately slow tempo

VARIATION
Changing the rhythm or notes of a theme to create variety.

EIGHTH-NOTE EXPRESS

32

Count: 1 & 2 & 3 & 4 &

RHYTHM RIDDLE

Clap first, then play.

33

BILE THEM CABBAGE DOWN

Allegro

American Fiddle Tune

34

SURPRISE SYMPHONY

THEME
Andante

Franz Joseph Haydn
(1732–1809)

35

VARIATION

ACCENT ON CREATIVITY: *Variation on Lightly Row*

Create your own variation by changing some of the quarter notes into pairs of eighth notes.

German Folk Song

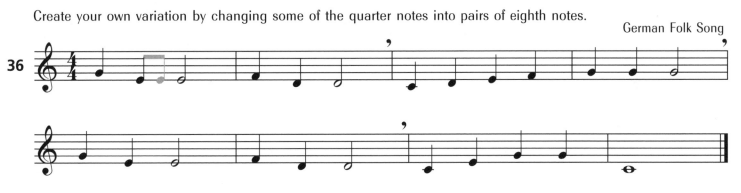

36

INTERNAL REPEAT

Repeat only the music between the signs.

1ST AND 2ND ENDINGS

2nd time: skip the first ending and play the second.

CLIMBING HIGHER

37

MORE EIGHTH NOTES

38

LONDON BRIDGE (Duet)

Moderato

English Folk Song

39

STODOLA PUMPA

Czech Folk Song

Allegro

40

SKIP TO MY LOU

American Folk Song

Moderato

41

FIRST CHORALE

Andante

42

ACCENT ON FRENCH HORN

43

For more individual technique practice, see page 42, #2.

SLUR

"Too"

Connects notes of different pitch.

Tongue only the first note.

DOTTED HALF NOTE

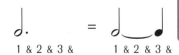

1 & 2 & 3 &   1 & 2 & 3 &

A dot following a note increases its length by ½ its original value.

In ¾ and ⁴⁄₄ time, a dotted half note receives 3 beats.

DIVISI

div.

Some players play the top notes while others play the bottom notes.

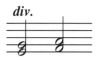

TIME SIGNATURE

3 = 3 beats in each measure
4 = quarter note receives 1 beat

SLURS AND DOTS

44

THREE-FOUR DUET

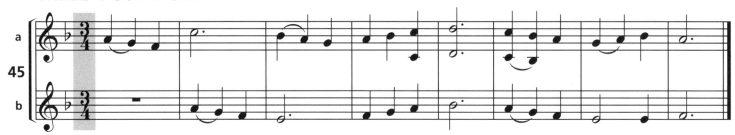

a
45
b

SOUTHERN ROSES

Johann Strauss, Jr.
(1825–1899)

Moderato

46

MEXICAN JUMPING BEANS

(Variation on CHIAPANECAS)

Mexican Folk Song

Allegro

47

1.   2.   *div.*

ACCENT ON THEORY

Draw the correct bar lines, then play.

48

SLUR

"Too"

Connects notes of different pitch. Tongue only the first note.

DOTTED HALF NOTE

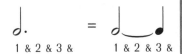

1 & 2 & 3 &   1 & 2 & 3 &

A dot following a note increases its length by ½ its original value.

In **3/4** and **4/4** time, a dotted half note receives 3 beats.

DIVISI

Some players play the top notes while others play the bottom notes.

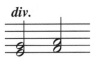

TIME SIGNATURE

3 = 3 beats in each measure
4 = quarter note receives 1 beat

SLURS AND DOTS

44

THREE-FOUR DUET

45

a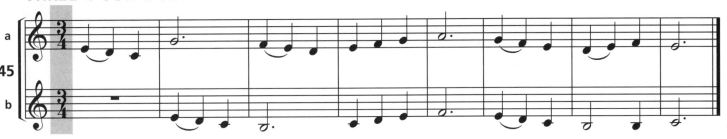

b

SOUTHERN ROSES

Johann Strauss, Jr.
(1825–1899)

Moderato

46

MEXICAN JUMPING BEANS
(Variation on CHIAPANECAS)

Allegro

Mexican Folk Song

47

ACCENT ON THEORY

Draw the correct bar lines, then play.

48

NATURAL

Cancels a flat or sharp until the next bar line.

KEY SIGNATURE

This key signature contains no sharps or flats.

DYNAMIC MARKINGS

f forte—loud *p* piano—soft

TWO WAYS TO PLAY IT

49

AURA LEE (Duet)

Andante

American Folk Song

50

FRÈRE JACQUES (Round)

Moderato

French Folk Song

51

MORNING from "PEER GYNT"

Andante

Edvard Grieg
(1843–1907)

52

ACCENT ON CREATIVITY: *Camptown Races*

Add your own dynamic markings, then perform.

Stephen Foster
(1826–1864)

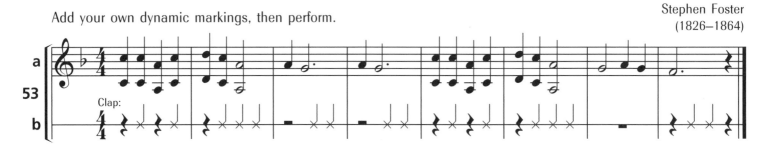

53

Clap:

SHARP

Raises the pitch of a note one half step.

KEY SIGNATURE

All F's should be played as F♯ throughout.

DYNAMIC MARKINGS

f **forte**—loud   *p* **piano**—soft

F♯
2
(1 2)

TWO WAYS TO PLAY IT

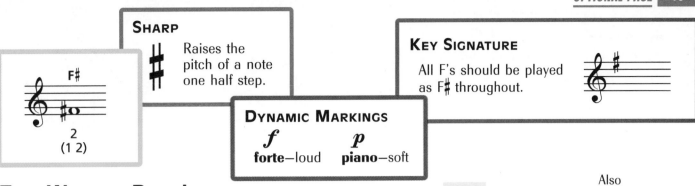

F♯   Also F♯

49

AURA LEE (Duet)

American Folk Song

Andante

a

50

b

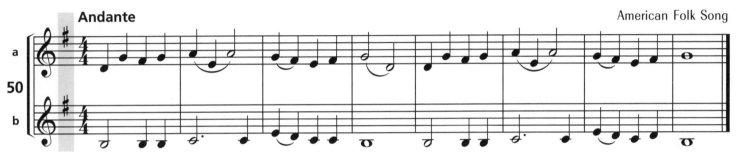

FRÈRE JACQUES (Round)

French Folk Song

Moderato   ①

51   *f*   *p*   *f*   *p*

②   ③   *f*   *p*   *f*   *p*

MORNING from "PEER GYNT"

Edvard Grieg
(1843–1907)

Andante

52   *p*

ACCENT ON CREATIVITY: *Camptown Races*

Stephen Foster
(1826–1864)

Add your own dynamic markings, then perform.

a

53

Clap:

b

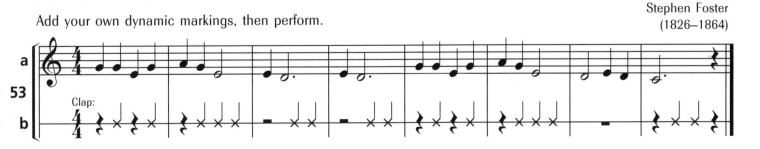

RITARDANDO
rit.
Gradually slow down the tempo.

FERMATA
Hold the note longer.

PICK-UP NOTES
(1 2 3) 4
Notes that precede the first full measure.

PATTERNS WITH PICK-UPS

54

(1 2 3) 4

CARNIVAL OF VENICE
Italian Folk Song

Moderato

55

(1 2) 3

JOLLY OLD ST. NICHOLAS
Traditional Carol

Allegro

56

THE SNAKE CHARMER
Traditional

Andante

57

rit.

BILL GROGAN'S GOAT
American Folk Song

Allegro

58

(1) 2 3 4

ACCENT ON FRENCH HORN

59

For more individual technique practice, see page 42, #3 & 4.

ACCENT ON PERFORMANCE

EAGLE SUMMIT MARCH

John O'Reilly and
Mark Williams

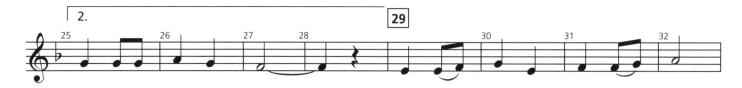

Accent on Performance

Eagle Summit March

John O'Reilly and
Mark Williams

Allegro

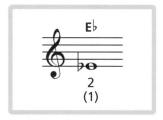

KEY SIGNATURE

All B's and E's should be played as B♭ and E♭ throughout.

ANOTHER NEW NOTE

WHEN LOVE IS KIND

Irish Folk Song

THEME FROM "SYMPHONY NO. 1"

Johannes Brahms
(1833–1897)

ALOHA 'OE

Queen Lili'uokalani (Hawaii)
(1838–1917)

MINKA, MINKA

Ukrainian Folk Song

ACCENT ON THEORY

KEY RINGS: Circle all notes changed by the key signature.

Bb
1
(T 1)

FLAT
Lowers the pitch of a note one half step.

KEY SIGNATURE
All B's should be played as Bb throughout.

ANOTHER NEW NOTE

60

WHEN LOVE IS KIND

Irish Folk Song

Moderato

61

THEME FROM "SYMPHONY NO. 1"

Johannes Brahms
(1833–1897)

Allegro

1.   2.

62

ALOHA 'OE

Queen Lili'uokalani (Hawaii)
(1838–1917)

Andante

63

MINKA, MINKA

Ukrainian Folk Song

Moderato

a

64

Clap:

b

ACCENT ON THEORY

KEY RINGS: Circle all notes changed by the key signature.

65

ACCENT >

Play the note stronger.

ORCHESTRATION

Choosing which instruments play a section of music.

THE KEY MAKES THE DIFFERENCE

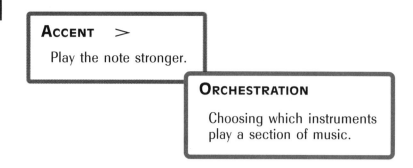

66

JASMINE FLOWER

Moderato

Chinese Folk Song

67

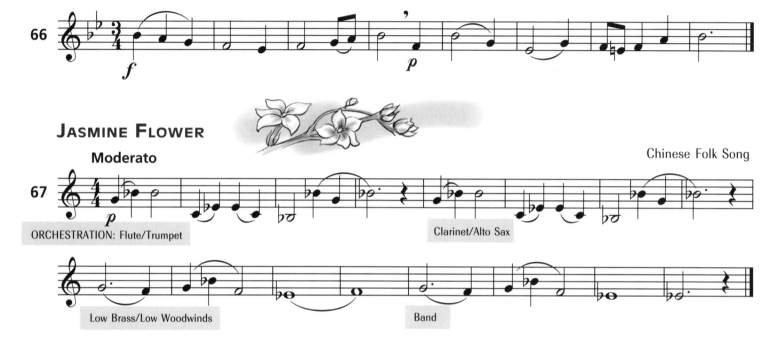

ORCHESTRATION: Flute/Trumpet

Clarinet/Alto Sax

Low Brass/Low Woodwinds

Band

BLUES ADVENTURE (Duet)

Allegro

68

a

b

a

b

ACCENT ON CREATIVITY: *This Old Man*

Choose your own orchestration for this melody.

American Folk Song

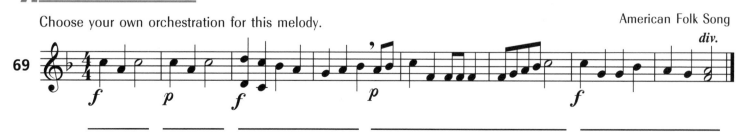

69

NATURAL
Cancels a flat or sharp until the next bar line.

ACCENT >
Play the note stronger.

ORCHESTRATION
Choosing which instruments play a section of music.

THE KEY MAKES THE DIFFERENCE

JASMINE FLOWER

Moderato

Chinese Folk Song

ORCHESTRATION: Flute/Trumpet

Clarinet/Alto Sax

Low Brass/Low Woodwinds

Band

BLUES ADVENTURE (Duet)

Allegro

ACCENT ON CREATIVITY: *This Old Man*

Choose your own orchestration for this melody.

American Folk Song

SINGLE EIGHTH NOTE AND EIGHTH REST

Each receives ½ beat in ²⁄₄, ³⁄₄ and ⁴⁄₄ time.

1 & 2 &

EASY EIGHTHS

70

POLLY WOLLY DOODLE

American Folk Song

Allegro

71

MARCH FROM "RONDO ALLA TURCA"

Wolfgang A. Mozart
(1756–1791)

Moderato

72

LA BAMBA

Mexican Folk Song

Allegro

73

div.

ACCENT ON FRENCH HORN

74

For more individual technique practice, see page 42, #5.

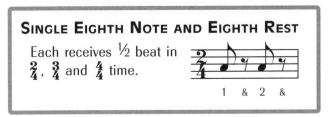

SINGLE EIGHTH NOTE AND EIGHTH REST

Each receives ½ beat in
2/4, **3/4** and **4/4** time.

1 & 2 &

EASY EIGHTHS

70

POLLY WOLLY DOODLE

American Folk Song

Allegro

71

MARCH FROM "RONDO ALLA TURCA"

Wolfgang A. Mozart
(1756–1791)

Moderato

72

LA BAMBA

Mexican Folk Song

Allegro

73

div.

ACCENT ON FRENCH HORN

74

For more individual technique practice, see page 42, #5.

TEMPO MARKING
Vivace
Very fast tempo

OPPOSITE DIRECTIONS

75

ACCIDENTAL ENCOUNTER

76

CHESTER

William Billings
(1746–1800)

Andante

77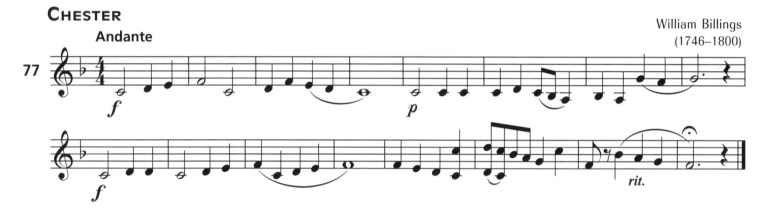

BELLA BIMBA

Italian Folk Song

Moderato

78

CHOPSTICKS (Duet)

Traditional

Vivace

79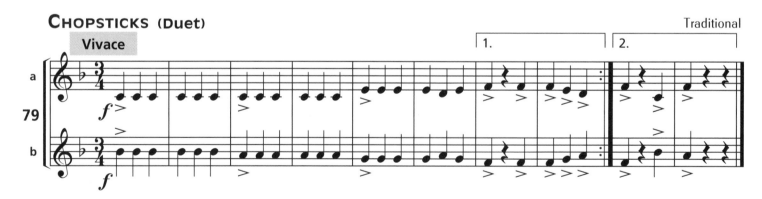

ACCENT ON THEORY Fill in the note names, then fill in the fingerings.

80

Note name: ___   ___   ___   ___   ___   ___

Fingering: _____   _____   _____   _____   _____   _____

B C
2 0
(T 2) (T 0)

TEMPO MARKING
Vivace
Very fast tempo

OPPOSITE DIRECTIONS

ACCIDENTAL ENCOUNTER

CHESTER

William Billings
(1746–1800)

BELLA BIMBA

Italian Folk Song

CHOPSTICKS (Duet)

Traditional

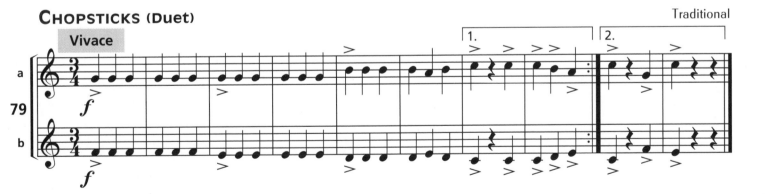

ACCENT ON THEORY

Fill in the note names, then fill in the fingerings.

Note name: ____   ____   ____   ____   ____   ____

Fingering: ____   ____   ____   ____   ____   ____

DYNAMIC MARKINGS

mf   **mezzo forte**—medium loud

mp   **mezzo piano**—medium soft

MULTIPLE MEASURE REST

Count: **1** 2 3 4 ⋮ **2** 2 3 4

FADING AWAY

EXTENDED RESTS (Duet)

KOOKABURRA (Round)

Australian Folk Song

FINALE FROM "ORPHEUS" (Can-Can)

Jacques Offenbach
(1819–1880)

ACCENT ON CREATIVITY: *Rhythmic Improvisation*

Improvise your own rhythms in each measure using only the pitches shown.

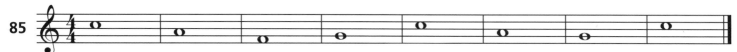

STACCATO ♩ Play the note ½ its normal length.

♩ ♩ = ♪ 𝄽 ♪ 𝄽

TONE BUILDER

86

A SHORT STORY

87

WILLIAM TELL OVERTURE

Gioacchino Rossini
(1792–1868)

88

Vivace

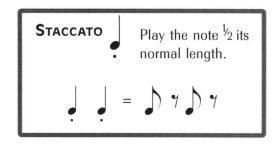

HATIKVAH

Israeli National Anthem

89

Andante

MINUET

Johann Sebastian Bach
(1685–1750)

90

Moderato

1.

2.

ACCENT ON FRENCH HORN

91

For more individual technique practice, see page 43, #6 & 7.

DOTTED QUARTERS

Count: 1 & 2 & 3 & 4 &

ANVIL CHORUS from "IL TROVATORE" (Duet)

Giuseppe Verdi (1813–1901)

Moderato

ALOUETTE

French-Canadian Folk Song

Vivace

SAKURA

Japanese Folk Song

Andante

WEARING OF THE GREEN

Irish Folk Song

Allegro

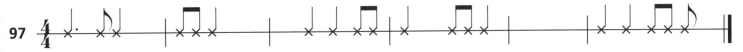

ACCENT ON THEORY

TAKE A REST: Complete each measure by adding the correct rest, then write in the counting and clap.

D.S. (DAL SEGNO) AL FINE
Go back to the sign 𝄋 and
play until **Fine**.

CLARINET CLIMB

98

IT'S RAINING, IT'S POURING

Traditional

ARIRANG

Korean Folk Song

ODE TO JOY from "SYMPHONY NO. 9"

Ludwig van Beethoven
(1770–1827)

ACCENT ON CREATIVITY: *Free Improvisation*

102

Using the five pitches shown, improvise your own melody
using any rhythms you know. You may play these notes
in any order, repeat notes or use rests.

For more individual technique practice, see page 43, #8.

SYNCOPATION

Starting a note that is one beat or longer on "&."

RHYTHM ANTICS

Count: 1 & 2 & 1 & 2 &

LONG TIME AGO

American Folk Song

Allegro

HAIL, THE CONQUERING HERO (Duet)

George F. Handel
(1685–1759)

Moderato

FOLK FESTIVAL

Moderato

WE WISH YOU A MERRY CHRISTMAS (Duet)

Traditional Carol

Vivace

ACCENT ON THEORY

114 Arrange the following tempo markings in order from slowest to fastest:

Moderato, Allegro, Andante, Vivace, Largo

_____ _____ _____ _____ _____

slowest - → fastest

ᴀCCENT ON PERFORMANCE

Wʜᴇɴ ᴛʜᴇ Sᴀɪɴᴛs Gᴏ Mᴀʀᴄʜɪɴɢ Iɴ

Arr. by John O'Reilly
and Mark Williams

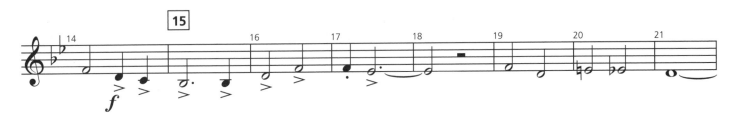

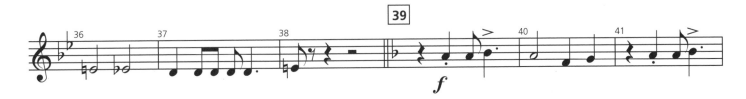

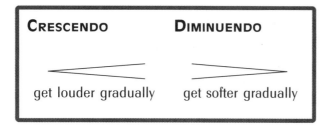

CRESCENDO | DIMINUENDO

get louder gradually | get softer gradually

CROSSING THE BREAK

115 ...

KUM BA YAH

Largo — African Folk Song

116 ...

TRUMPET VOLUNTARY (Duet)

Jeremiah Clarke (1674–1707)

Moderato

117 ...

FINLANDIA

Jean Sibelius (1865–1957)

Andante

118 ...

ACCENT ON CREATIVITY Create your own composition containing a balance of unity and variety.

119 ...

1. Copy the first two measures into measures 5 and 6 to create unity.
2. Compose new music for the remaining measures to add variety.
3. Play your composition.

TIME SIGNATURE 𝄴

Common Time—same as 4/4

SHEPHERD'S HEY (Duet)

English Folk Song

Allegro

BOTANY BAY

Australian Folk Song

Moderato

REUBEN AND RACHEL (Round)

Traditional

Vivace

AMAZING GRACE

American Folk Song

Andante

ACCENT ON FRENCH HORN

For more individual technique practice, see page 43, #9.

MORE SYNCOPATION

SYNCOPATED RHYTHMS

125   *mf*

Count: 1 & 2 & 3 & 4 &

RUSSIAN SAILOR'S DANCE

Reinhold Gliere
(1875–1956)

Moderato

126   *f*

YE BANKS AND BRAES OF BONNIE DOON (Duet)

Scottish Folk Song

Andante

a
127
b

TOM DOOLEY

Allegro

American Folk Song

128   *mf*

A CCENT ON THEORY   Arrange the following dynamics in order from softest to loudest and back: *mf*, *p*,

f, *mp*.

129

MIXIN' IT UP

130

ON TOP OF OLD SMOKY

Allegro

American Folk Song

131

Peter I. Tchaikovsky
(1840–1893)

MARCH SLAV

Largo

132

LAS MAÑANITAS

Moderato

Mexican Folk Song

133

POMP AND CIRCUMSTANCE

Andante

Edward Elgar
(1857–1934)

134

For more individual technique practice, see page 43, #10.

FRENCH HORN SOLO

POLOVETSIAN DANCE
from PRINCE IGOR

Alexander Borodin
(1833–1887)

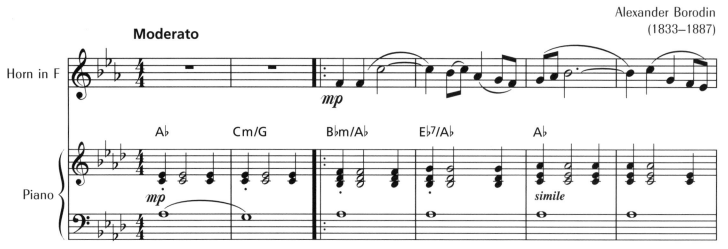

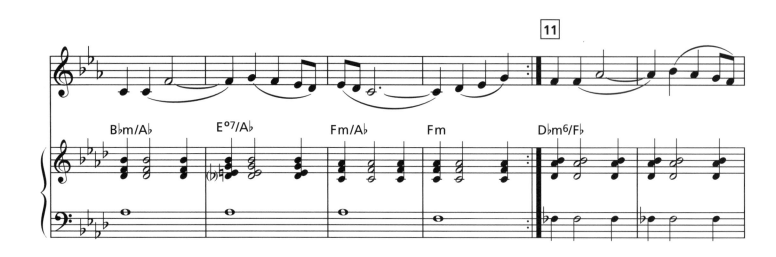

ACCENT ON PERFORMANCE

SOUSA SPECTACULAR

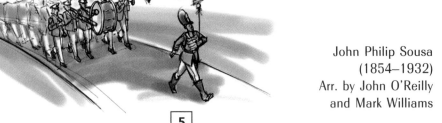

John Philip Sousa
(1854–1932)
Arr. by John O'Reilly
and Mark Williams

ACCENT ON SCALES

F MAJOR SCALE AND CHORDS (Concert B♭)

C MAJOR SCALE AND CHORDS (Concert F)

B♭ MAJOR SCALE AND CHORDS (Concert E♭)

E♭ MAJOR SCALE AND CHORDS (Concert A♭)

F MAJOR SCALE IN THIRDS (Concert B♭)

Optional
articulations:

C MAJOR SCALE IN THIRDS (Concert F)

B♭ MAJOR SCALE IN THIRDS (Concert E♭)

E♭ MAJOR SCALE IN THIRDS (Concert A♭)

CHROMATIC SCALE

ACCENT ON RHYTHMS

ACCENT ON RESTS

ACCENT ON FRENCH HORN

ACCENT ON CHORALES

CONCERT Bb

Andante

CONCERT F

Largo

CONCERT Eb

Andante

CONCERT Ab

Andante

GLOSSARY

ACCENT (>) Play the note stronger

ALLEGRO Fast tempo

ANDANTE Moderately slow tempo

BACH, JOHANN SEBASTIAN German composer (1685–1750)

BAR LINE Divides the staff into measures

BASS CLEF (𝄢) Also called F clef. The fourth line of the staff is the note F

BEETHOVEN, LUDWIG VAN German composer (1770–1827)

BILLINGS, WILLIAM American composer (1746–1800)

BRAHMS, JOHANNES German composer (1833–1897)

BREATH MARK (ʼ) A suggested place to take a breath

CLARKE, JEREMIAH English composer (1674–1707)

COMMON TIME (𝄴) Same as $\frac{4}{4}$ time signature

CRESCENDO (⟨) Get louder gradually

D.C. (DA CAPO) AL FINE Go back to the beginning and play until Fine

DIMINUENDO (⟩) Get softer gradually

DIVISI Some players play the top notes while others play the bottom notes

DOUBLE BAR (𝄂) The end of a section of music

D.S. (DAL SEGNO) AL FINE Go back to the sign 𝄋 and play until Fine

DUET A composition with parts for two players

DVOŘÁK, ANTONIN Czech composer (1841–1904)

DYNAMIC MARKINGS Symbols that indicate loudness or softness of the music

ELGAR, EDWARD English composer (1857–1934)

FERMATA (𝄐) Hold the note longer

1ST AND 2ND ENDINGS Play the 1st ending first time through, then on the repeat, skip to the 2nd ending

FLAT (♭) Lowers the pitch of a note one half step

FORTE (*f*) Loud

FOSTER, STEPHEN American composer (1826–1864)

GLIERE, REINHOLD Russian composer (1875–1956)

GRIEG, EDVARD Norwegian composer (1843–1907)

HANDEL, GEORGE F. English composer of German birth (1685–1759)

HAYDN, FRANZ JOSEPH Austrian composer (1732–1809)

HUMPERDINCK, ENGELBERT German composer (1854–1921)

INTERNAL REPEAT Repeat only the music between the signs

KEY SIGNATURE Indicates notes which are to be flatted or sharped throughout

LARGO Very slow

LEDGER LINES Used to extend the staff

LILIʼUOKALANI Hawaiian composer (1838–1917)

MEASURE The distance between two bar lines

MEZZO FORTE (*mf*) Medium loud

MEZZO PIANO (*mp*) Medium soft

MODERATO Medium tempo

MOZART, WOLFGANG A. Austrian composer (1756–1791)

MULTIPLE MEASURE REST Indicates more than one measure of rest

NATURAL (♮) Cancels a flat or sharp until the next bar line

OFFENBACH, JACQUES French composer (1819–1880)

ORCHESTRATION Choosing which instruments play a section of music

PIANO (*p*) Soft

PICK-UP NOTE(S) Note(s) preceding the first full measure

REPEAT SIGN Play the music again from the beginning

RITARDANDO (RIT.) Gradually slow down the tempo

ROSSINI, GIOACCHINO Italian composer (1792–1868)

ROUND Playing the same music beginning at different times

SHARP (♯) Raises the pitch of a note one half step

SIBELIUS, JEAN Finnish composer (1865–1957)

SLUR Connects notes of different pitch

SOLO One person playing

SOUSA, JOHN PHILIP American composer (1854–1932)

STACCATO (·) Play the note ½ its normal length

STAFF 5 lines and 4 spaces used for writing music

STRAUSS, JOHANN JR. Austrian composer (1825–1899)

SYNCOPATION Starting a note that is one beat or longer on "&"

TCHAIKOVSKY, PETER I. Russian composer (1840–1893)

TEMPO MARKINGS Terms which indicate the speed of the music

TIE Joins two notes of the same pitch to make one long note

TIME SIGNATURE Indicates how many beats are in each measure and what kind of note receives one beat

TREBLE CLEF (𝄞) Also called G clef. The second line of the staff is the note G

VARIATION Changing the rhythm or notes of a theme to create variety

VERDI, GIUSEPPE Italian composer (1813–1901)

VIVACE Very fast tempo

FRENCH HORN FINGERING CHART

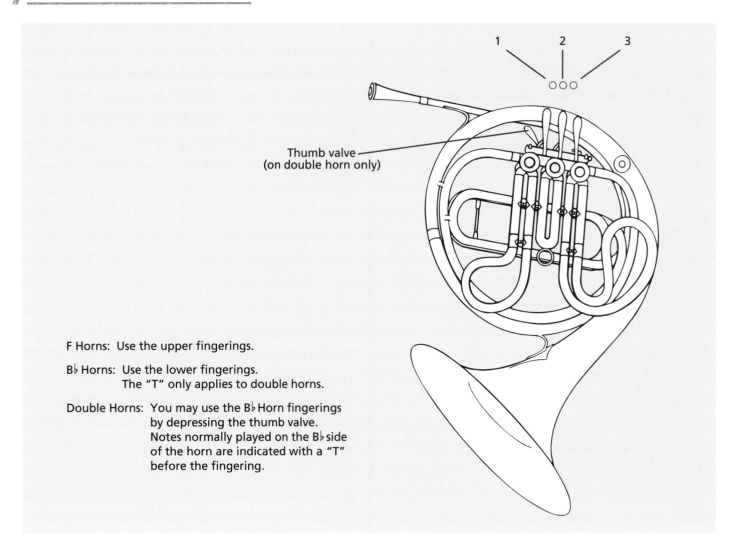

1   **2**   **3**

Thumb valve
(on double horn only)

F Horns: Use the upper fingerings.

B♭ Horns: Use the lower fingerings.
The "T" only applies to double horns.

Double Horns: You may use the B♭ Horn fingerings
by depressing the thumb valve.
Notes normally played on the B♭ side
of the horn are indicated with a "T"
before the fingering.

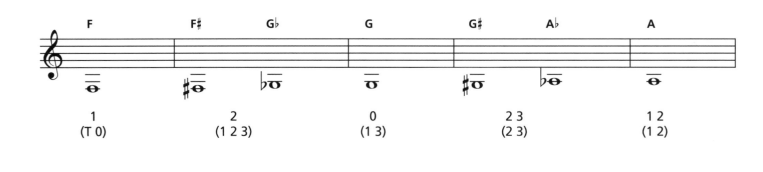

F	F♯	G♭	G	G♯	A♭	A
1	2		0	2 3		1 2
(T 0)	(1 2 3)		(1 3)	(2 3)		(1 2)

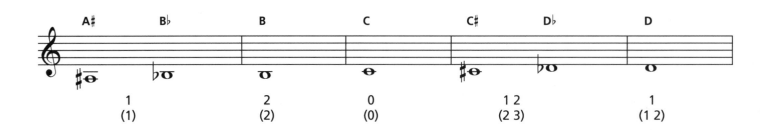

A♯	B♭	B	C	C♯	D♭	D
1		2	0	1 2		1
(1)		(2)	(0)	(2 3)		(1 2)

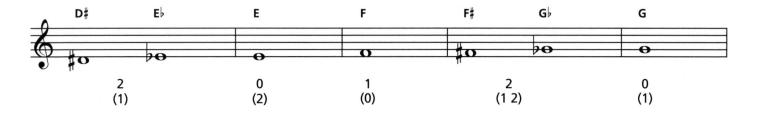

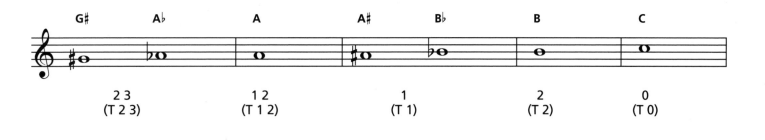

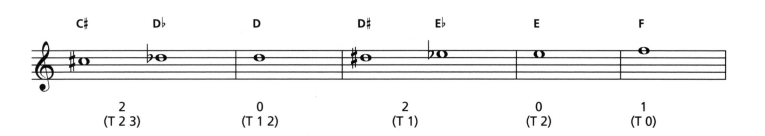

HOME PRACTICE RECORD

Week	Date	ASSIGNMENT	Mon	Tue	Wed	Thur	Fri	Sat	Sun	Total	Parent Signature
1											
2											
3											
4											
5											
6											
7											
8											
9											
10											
11											
12											
13											
14											
15											
16											
17											
18											
19											
20											
21											
22											
23											
24											
25											
26											
27											
28											
29											
30											
31											
32											
33											
34											
35											
36	Date	ASSIGNMENT	Mon	Tue	Wed	Thur	Fri	Sat	Sun	Total	